Rough Rider

The Challenge of Moto-Cross

Written by   C. J. Naden

Troll Associates

Library of Congress Catalog Card Number: 79-52177
ISBN 0-89375-250-9   (0-89375-251-7 soft cover ed.)

*Photo credits: Steve Foitl, Mary Grothe, Daytona International Speedway,
Peter Magoon, Cycle Guide*

A moto-cross start at Daytona.

They come at you looking like the defensive line of a pro football team—on wheels! They don't play football, but they *are* pros. And this is not a ball game. It is the start of a professional moto-cross race. Moto-cross is perhaps the roughest, toughest of all motorcycle contests. It is also one of the most popular.

Over a jump...

Moto-cross racing is a lot faster than football—and just as rugged. So the riders dress for it. They wear special boots, gloves, shoulder pads, helmets, face guards, shin pads, and jerseys with numbers on them.

...and into a berm!

Why all this safety gear? Because a moto-cross race is held on rough, natural ground. There are berms—hills of dirt pushed up by the cycle wheels. There are gullies, sand traps, water traps, ruts, holes, rocks, mud, cliffs, and jumps. Sometimes other hazards are added to make the race still more difficult.

Even on such a rugged course, moto-cross riders may hit speeds of about 128 kilometers per hour (80 miles per hour). A spill here means bruises and lumps for sure, and maybe worse. And it means a lot of time in the air! So the riders need all the protection they can get.

...and back on the track.

Moto-cross racing began in Great Britain, but France gave the sport its name. In French, *moto-cross* means "cross-country motorcycling." In a cross-country race, the length of the course may be anywhere from 80 kilometers (50 miles) to several hundred. A moto-cross track is about 1.6 kilometers (1 mile) in length.

Around the first lap.

In a cross-country race, the riders go from start to finish just
once. But in a moto-cross, the riders must complete a certain
number of laps around the closed, rough track. This makes it
easier for spectators to see all the action and excitement.

Slowing down at the turns.

The moto-cross track is often very narrow. Many riders battle for the same spot at the same time! That's one of the things that make moto-cross so exciting to watch. The riders may hit high speeds on the rough and bumpy circuit. But they must slow down at the turns.

Today's riders are younger than ever.

The first moto-cross in Great Britain was held in the early 1920s. It did not look very much like the moto-cross races of today. Unlike today, the cyclists were all English gentlemen in sporty tweed jackets and caps. They tried, without great success, to move their too-heavy machines up and down the hillsides. The race was like a big family outing.

Rough, bumpy terrain in a modern race.

The next English moto-cross was 48 kilometers (30 miles) long! The race was held in two parts—one lap around the course in the morning and another in the afternoon. That allowed the riders to break for lunch. The winner was the rider with the fastest average time for the two laps.

Trying for the most laps.

Today's moto-cross riders don't take time out for lunch, but the race is still divided into sections. These sections, or short races, are called *motos*. Usually there are three. Each moto may last from 15 to 45 minutes. The rider who completes the most laps in that time wins the highest number of points for that moto.

Bales of hay offer some protection.

To win a moto-cross, you must have the highest points after all three motos. So, it is possible for one rider to win the first two motos, but badly lose the third—and so lose the race. That's why moto-cross is said to be about the toughest of all motorcycle contests. You have to be tough just to last through all three motos!

Spectators watch the action in all kinds of weather.

What does it take to be a top moto-cross rider? It takes toughness and strength to go the distance over this bone-rattling course. It takes quick reactions and steely nerves. It takes brain power to figure the quickest and best way to ride the race—rain or shine.

One of today's moto-cross bikes.

Moto-cross cycles are special. They have to be, to stand the beating! The cycles used in early races were just too heavy, and their engines too weak, to get through mud or up slippery hills. And they were hard to control. The rider had to worry more about staying on the bike than winning the race!

Taking a beating.

Today's winning moto-cross bike must be strong, powerful, and light in weight. It must be easy to handle, easy to control, and able to skim around hazards. It must be strong enough to take a long, hard beating. Imagine 45 straight minutes of bouncing up and down over rocks and dirt and holes!

Not the way to come down!

Sometimes a hard bump at high speed sends the bike and rider straight up in the air. The problem, of course, is not going up but coming down. Whatever they do, wherever they go, landing without a spill is one thing moto-cross riders had better learn!

Flying high—but losing!

Because the course is so rough, the riders spend an amazing amount of time in midair. Too much time in the air, with both wheels off the course, means lost minutes. And a lost race. Whenever possible, the rider wants to keep both tires touching the ground. That's where the power comes from. With the tires in the air, the engine is racing for nowhere.

The tires on moto-cross bikes look something like auto snow tires. They are made to grip the ground. The rider often checks the tires to get rid of stones picked up on the rough course. Even a small stone can cause the bike to swerve.

Each year there are thousands of amateur and professional motorcycle races, including moto-cross. A yearly series of moto-cross races, called the Trans AMA, is staged all over the United States. The races also draw many of the big-name European moto-cross stars.

...and over!

Each year in Europe, the top riders compete for the moto-cross world championship. The season runs from April to September. But most of the races are held in the summer months when the courses are likely to be hard and dry. Riders compete in classes according to engine size.

Big races bring the fans.

The big events on the championship circuit are called the Grand Prix Series. Most of them are run in Europe, but there are also races in the United States and Canada. Only the very best riders from each country are allowed to enter these contests. And all the moto-cross riders want to compete.

Some courses are hilly and dusty.

For many years, most of the top moto-cross riders have been Europeans. There are so many good riders in Europe, and so many races, that you must be very good to win. Also, European moto-cross tracks are each so different that the riders learn to win on any type of ground.

Some courses are flat and hard.

American courses are made of dirt, and are somewhat flat. But in Europe, the moto-cross tour may go from the deep, black sand of Holland, to the dusty mountain courses of Italy, to the rocky mounds of France, to the grassy hillsides of England. Each is a different and special challenge.

At the starting gate.

Moto-cross is popular with the fans for many reasons. For one thing, it is easy to watch. The courses are fairly short, and spectators can line up just about anywhere along them. Thousands and thousands of people attend moto-cross races. And today is the start of a big race.

Roaring around the turns.

They're off and away from the starting gate! The bikes burst into speed. The ground is dry and hard in some places. But there are water hazards and mud holes scattered about. Each rider is digging hard for the lead.

The fight for the lead.

With the deafening roar of many powerful engines, the riders
zoom past in a blur of color and a blast of noise. The wheels
spin, sending great swirls of dust and dirt into the dry summer
air. Soon the riders are almost lost in the dust cloud. Which one
will head the pack after this hairpin turn?

Now it's up and over a deep gully. Machine after machine leaps and twists in the air to keep balance and clear the jump. For a second or two, they seem to float like noisy birds. Then they hit the ground with a bounce that seems surely to break bones and machine. But on they go.

Leaping ahead!

The course leads up a grassy hillside. The spectators are held behind rope barriers. They eagerly wait to catch a first look at the numbers of the leaders. And what a sight as the pack charges around the bend, colored helmets bright in the sun! The riders zoom around the rough circuit again and again.

Knobby tires dig up even hard-packed dirt.

On and on they go. Through deep, flying sand and rock-filled gullies. They charge into the air and over a hill, down the straight, hard track. There is no time for a mistake here. The riders keep their eyes and minds always on the dangerous course. And the bikes always in full control. That's the only way to win.

Riders slow down for the yellow caution flag.

Dirt-streaked and water-splashed, the bikes roar on. The first moto is almost over. Some of the riders are out of the race already. Some are very far behind the leaders. It's a long after-noon, and there are two more motos to go!

But when the long day is over, home comes the mud-covered winner. And the thrill of victory is worth anything the course can dish out. Fans and riders both agree—this is perhaps the greatest of all motorcycle challenges. It is surely one of the roughest, toughest sports in all the world!